WELCOME TO THE U.S.A.
NEVADA

Written by Ann Heinrichs   Illustrated by Matt Kania
Content Adviser: Dr. Michael Green, Professor of History,
Community College of Southern Nevada, Las Vegas, Nevada

The Child's World

Published in the United States of America by The Child's World®
PO Box 326 • Chanhassen, MN 55317-0326
800-599-READ • www.childsworld.com

Photo Credits
Cover: Brand X Pictures; frontispiece: Medioimages.

Interior: Corbis: 14 (David Muench), 18 (Phil Schermeister), 26 (Lester Lefkowitz), 29 (Dan Lamont); Richard Cummins/Corbis: 6, 34; Getty Images/Stone/Paul Chesley: 33; Ronni Hannaman/Arlington Group: 17; Nevada Commission on Tourism: 9, 10, 13, 22; Photodisc: 25; Scott T. Smith/Corbis: 21, 30.

Acknowledgments
The Child's World®: Mary Berendes, Publishing Director

Editorial Directions, Inc.: E. Russell Primm, Editorial Director; Katie Marsico, Associate Editor; Judith Shiffer, Assistant Editor; Matt Messbarger, Editorial Assistant; Susan Hindman, Copy Editor; Melissa McDaniel, Proofreader; Kevin Cunningham, Peter Garnham, Matt Messbarger, Olivia Nellums, Chris Simms, Molly Symmonds, Katherine Trickle, Carl Stephen Wender, Fact Checkers; Tim Griffin/IndexServ, Indexer; Cian Loughlin O'Day, Photo Researcher and Editor

The Design Lab: Kathleen Petelinsek, Design; Julia Goozen, Art Production

Library of Congress Cataloging-in-Publication Data
Heinrichs, Ann.
  Nevada / by Ann Heinrichs ; cartography and illustrations by Matt Kania.
    p. cm. — (Welcome to the U.S.A.)
  Includes index.
  ISBN 1-59296-476-1 (library bound : alk. paper)
  1. Nevada—Juvenile literature. 2. Nevada—Geography—Juvenile literature. I. Kania, Matt, ill. II. Title.
  F841.3.H45 2005
  917.93—dc22   2005009588

Ann Heinrichs is the author of more than 100 books for children and young adults. She has also enjoyed successful careers as a children's book editor and an advertising copywriter. Ann grew up in Fort Smith, Arkansas, and lives in Chicago, Illinois.

About the Author
Ann Heinrichs

Matt Kania loves maps and, as a kid, dreamed of making them. In school he studied geography and cartography, and today he makes maps for a living. Matt's favorite thing about drawing maps is learning about the places they represent. Many of the maps he has created can be found in books, magazines, videos, Web sites, and public places.

About the
Map Illustrator
Matt Kania

On the cover: Don't forget to hike through scenic Red Rock Canyon!
On page one: Visit Reno! Learn why it's called the Biggest Little City in the World.

OUR NEVADA TRIP

Do you like adventure? Then you'll love your tour through Nevada! Just wait and see all you can do. You'll ride out on the range with cowboys. You'll watch a gunfight in a mining town. You'll hang out with mountain men. You'll stand atop a massive dam. You'll gaze up at red rock towers. And you'll watch jackrabbits and mountain goats scampering along.

What do you think? Shall we hit the road? Then buckle up and hang on tight. We're off to see Nevada!

WELCOME TO
NEVADA

As you travel through Nevada, watch for all the interesting facts along the way.

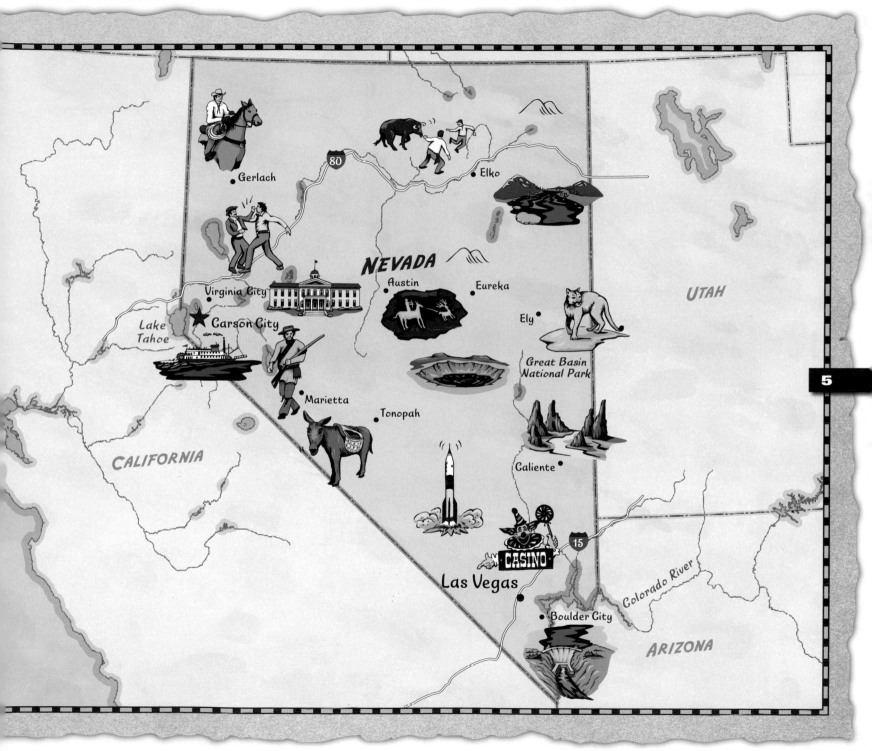

Nevada usually gets less rainfall than any other state.

Want a peek at some amazing rock formations?
Just tour Cathedral Gorge!

The Mojave Desert reaches into southwest Nevada from California. *Mojave* is pronounced "mo-HAH-vee."

The rocks are red, pink, white, and gray. Some have narrow openings you can squeeze through. Some are walls looming high overhead. Others are brightly colored towers and cliffs. You're wandering through Cathedral Gorge!

Nevada has many areas with strange rock formations. Most of Nevada lies in the Great Basin Region. That's a dry, rugged part of the country. Flat, sandy deserts cover much of the land.

Many small mountain ranges run through the state. Swift streams rush through their rocky canyons. The Sierra Nevada are mountains on the western border. Lake Tahoe rests high in a valley there.

Let's head up to the north end of the gorge. It's got some caves we can crawl through!

The name *Nevada* comes from a Spanish word meaning "snow-clad." That refers to Nevada's snowcapped mountains.

San Jacinto •

UTAH

Highest Temperature: Laughlin June 29, 1994 125°F (52°C)

Lowest Temperature: San Jacinto January 8, 1937 -50°F (-46°C)

CALIFORNIA

Lake Tahoe

Sierra Nevada

Great Basin Region

Boundary Peak

Caliente •

HIGHEST AND LOWEST POINTS
Highest: Boundary Peak at 13,140 feet (4,005 m)
Lowest: Along the Colorado River in Clark County at 470 feet (143 m)

The Valley of Fire is near Overton. Wind and water have worn its rocks into weird shapes. One rock is named Elephant Rock.

Clark County

Red Rock Canyon is southwest of Las Vegas. Many movies have been filmed among its spectacular rock formations.

Las Vegas •

Overton •

Mojave Desert

Colorado River

ARIZONA

The Colorado River forms part of the border between Nevada and Arizona.

Laughlin •

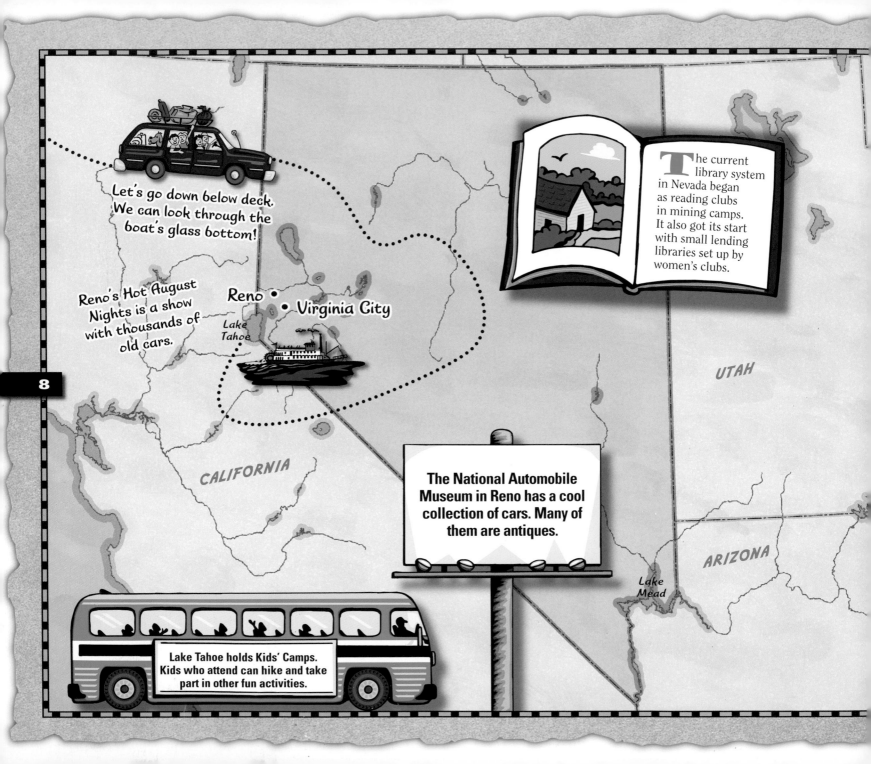

Let's go down below deck. We can look through the boat's glass bottom!

Reno's Hot August Nights is a show with thousands of old cars.

The current library system in Nevada began as reading clubs in mining camps. It also got its start with small lending libraries set up by women's clubs.

The National Automobile Museum in Reno has a cool collection of cars. Many of them are antiques.

Lake Tahoe holds Kids' Camps. Kids who attend can hike and take part in other fun activities.

Reno •
• Virginia City

Lake Tahoe

CALIFORNIA

UTAH

ARIZONA

Lake Mead

Paddleboating on Lake Tahoe

You're cruising around Lake Tahoe. Your boat is the *Tahoe Queen*. Its big paddle wheel turns around. That's how the boat moves through the water!

Lake Tahoe is a popular vacation spot in the Sierra Nevada. You can ride a **tram** high over the valley. In the winter, people go snowmobiling. They ski down the snow-covered slopes.

Lake Mead is another fun place. People enjoy swimming and waterskiing there. Some people like mountain climbing in Nevada. Others go hiking and look for wildlife.

Maybe you enjoy big cities. Or perhaps you prefer the outdoors. Whatever you like, you'll find it in Nevada!

Hang on tight! Try parasailing over Lake Tahoe!

The Virginia City International Camel Races are held in September.

The main entrance to Great Basin National Park is near Baker.

Great Basin National Park

These bighorn sheep call the Nevada desert home.

Nevada has many types of land. Each one is home to special animals. Great Basin National Park is fun to explore. It has both dry deserts and lush mountains. Many different kinds of animals live there.

Sagebrush grows in the park's desert areas. Here, jackrabbits and ground squirrels scurry along the ground. Pronghorn antelopes run swiftly across the plains.

Pine and juniper trees grow on higher ground. There you'll find mule deer. Near streams, you'll see weasels and ringtail cats.

Mountain lions live on the rugged mountain slopes. You might see bighorn sheep and mountain goats, too. They're expert rock climbers!

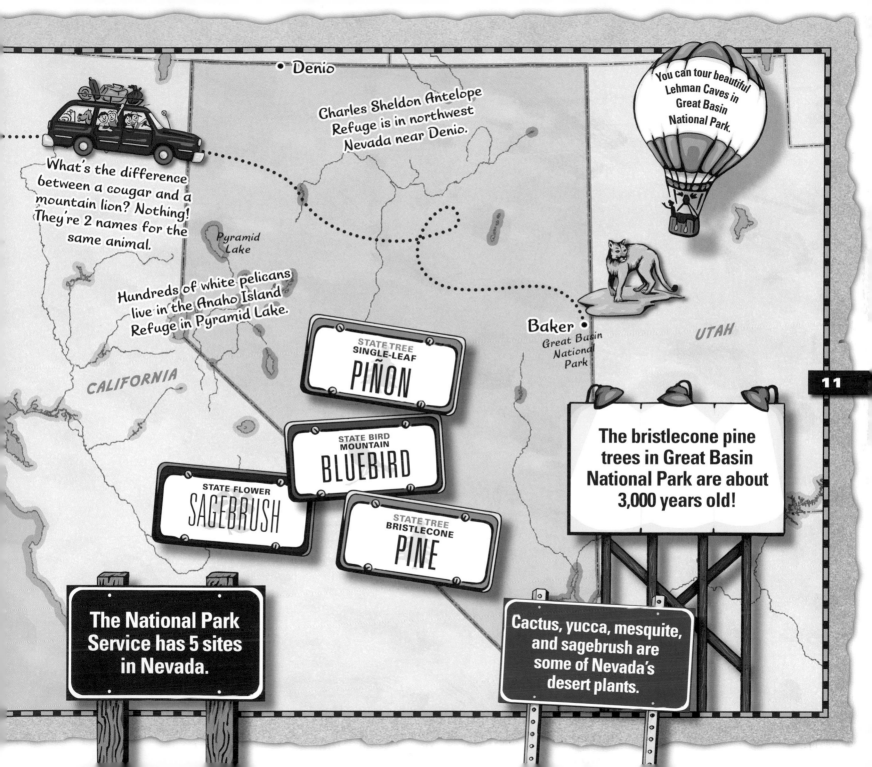

Denio

Charles Sheldon Antelope Refuge is in northwest Nevada near Denio.

You can tour beautiful Lehman Caves in Great Basin National Park.

What's the difference between a cougar and a mountain lion? Nothing! They're 2 names for the same animal.

Pyramid Lake

Hundreds of white pelicans live in the Anaho Island Refuge in Pyramid Lake.

CALIFORNIA

Baker
Great Basin National Park

UTAH

STATE TREE
SINGLE-LEAF
PIÑON

STATE BIRD
MOUNTAIN
BLUEBIRD

STATE FLOWER
SAGEBRUSH

STATE TREE
BRISTLECONE
PINE

The bristlecone pine trees in Great Basin National Park are about 3,000 years old!

The National Park Service has 5 sites in Nevada.

Cactus, yucca, mesquite, and sagebrush are some of Nevada's desert plants.

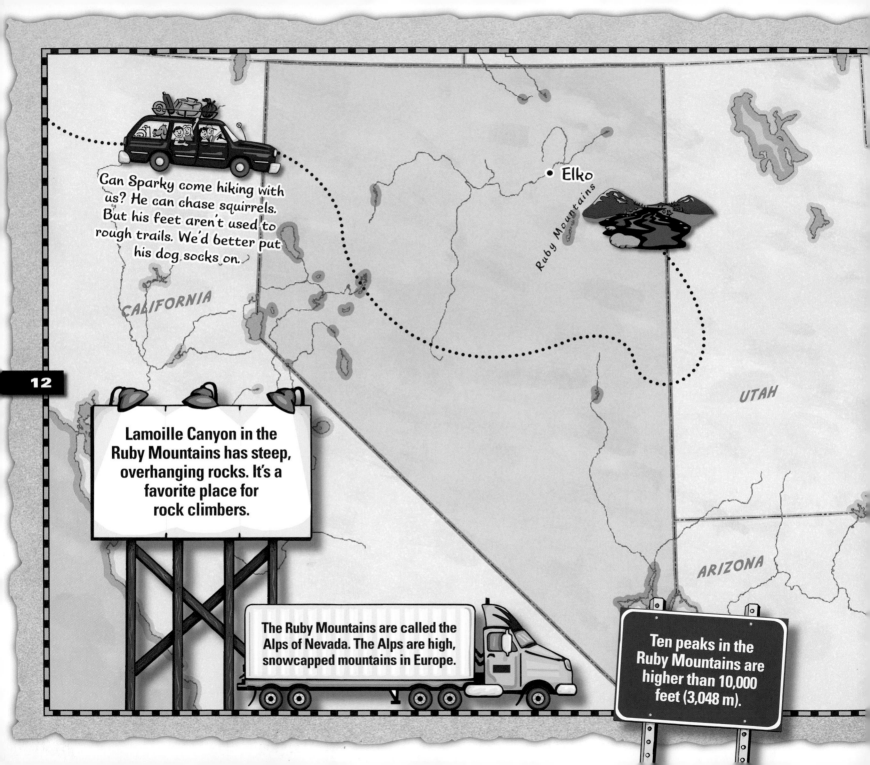

Can Sparky come hiking with us? He can chase squirrels. But his feet aren't used to rough trails. We'd better put his dog socks on.

Elko

Ruby Mountains

CALIFORNIA

UTAH

ARIZONA

Lamoille Canyon in the Ruby Mountains has steep, overhanging rocks. It's a favorite place for rock climbers.

The Ruby Mountains are called the Alps of Nevada. The Alps are high, snowcapped mountains in Europe.

Ten peaks in the Ruby Mountains are higher than 10,000 feet (3,048 m).

Exploring the Ruby Mountains

Many people think of Nevada as desert land. But they've never seen the Ruby Mountains!

These lush mountains are southeast of Elko. Their snowcapped peaks rise over green meadows. Sparkling blue lakes nestle in high valleys. Melting snow fills up the swift streams. The water rushes down the mountainsides.

Would you like to go hiking here? If you go, you'll meet lots of wildlife. Beavers, coyotes, and mule deer roam the forests. Mountain goats and bighorn sheep live here, too. You might see skunks or porcupines waddling along. Watch out! Don't get too close to either type of animal!

Moo! Lamoille Canyon is also good for grazing cattle.

Want to view some ancient art? Check out the petroglyphs at Hickison Point.

Sloan Canyon National Conservation Area is near Las Vegas. It has about 1,700 petroglyphs.

Petroglyphs at Hickison Point

Head up the mountain at Hickison Point. It's about halfway between Austin and Eureka. Soon you'll see dozens of petroglyphs. Those are drawings carved into rock. Can you figure out what the pictures are?

Ancient people carved these drawings. They could be scenes of hunting activities. Nevada has many other petroglyph sites. American Indians lived there hundreds of years ago. Some people made their homes in caves. Others built pueblos. These dwellings were like apartment buildings.

Spanish explorers may have crossed Nevada in the 1700s. They didn't settle down, though.

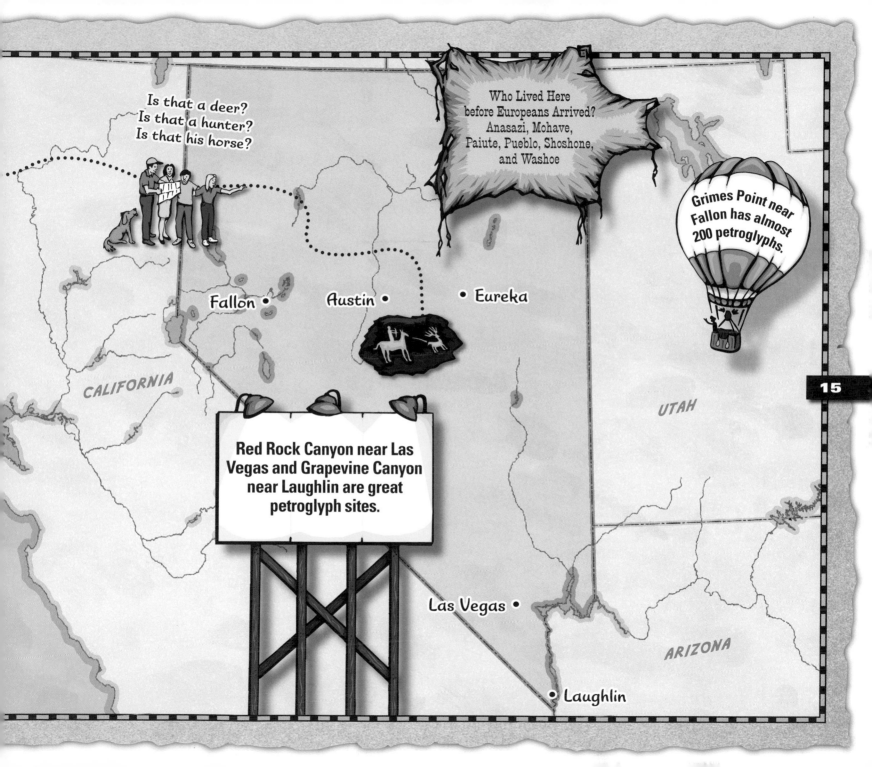

Is that a deer?
Is that a hunter?
Is that his horse?

Who Lived Here before Europeans Arrived? Anasazi, Mohave, Paiute, Pueblo, Shoshone, and Washoe

Grimes Point near Fallon has almost 200 petroglyphs.

Fallon •

Austin •

• Eureka

CALIFORNIA

UTAH

Red Rock Canyon near Las Vegas and Grapevine Canyon near Laughlin are great petroglyph sites.

Las Vegas •

ARIZONA

• Laughlin

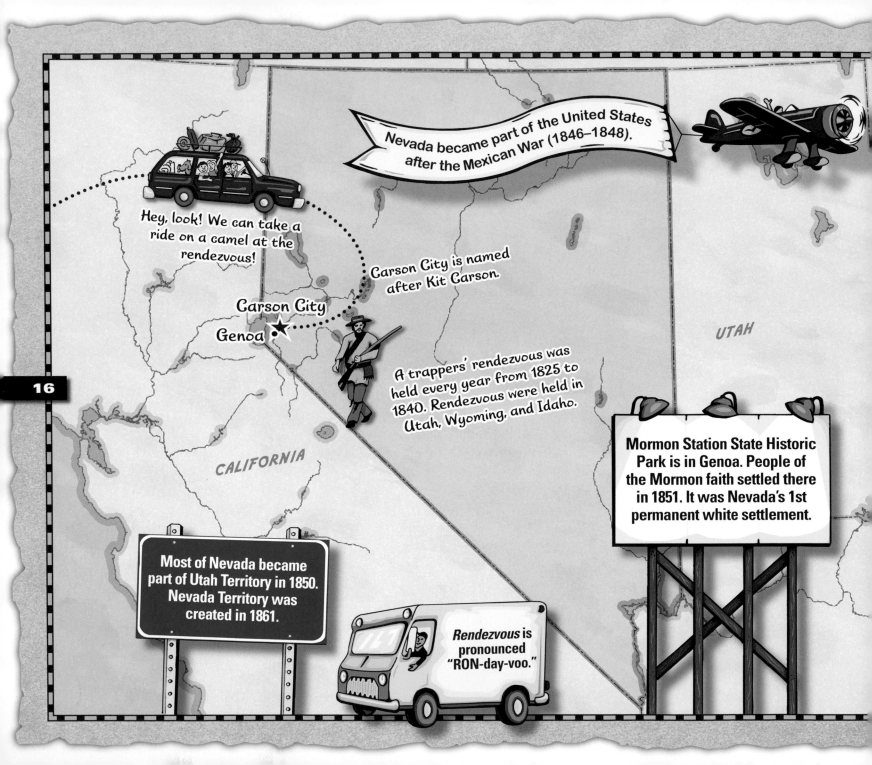

Nevada became part of the United States after the Mexican War (1846–1848).

Hey, look! We can take a ride on a camel at the rendezvous!

Carson City is named after Kit Carson.

Carson City

Genoa

A trappers' rendezvous was held every year from 1825 to 1840. Rendezvous were held in Utah, Wyoming, and Idaho.

UTAH

CALIFORNIA

Mormon Station State Historic Park is in Genoa. People of the Mormon faith settled there in 1851. It was Nevada's 1st permanent white settlement.

Most of Nevada became part of Utah Territory in 1850. Nevada Territory was created in 1861.

Rendezvous is pronounced "RON-day-voo."

The Carson City Rendezvous

Dress like a **pioneer.** Camp out with the mountain men. Watch some Native American dances. It's the Carson City Rendezvous!

Fur trappers were Nevada's early explorers. They began arriving in the 1820s. Peter Ogden and Jedediah Smith came first. John C. Frémont began exploring Nevada in 1843. His guide was the famous **scout** Kit Carson.

Trappers and Indians got together once a year. They held a rendezvous, or big meeting. They traded, told stories, and played games. Come to the rendezvous and join the fun!

Is this Kit Carson? No! The Carson City Rendezvous features costumed actors.

Explorer John C. Frémont was a U.S. Army officer.

Hot Times in Virginia City

Watch out! The gunfighters are ready to draw. Bang! One of them falls to the ground. Until he gets back up, that is. You're watching a gunfight show in Virginia City!

Virginia City was once a pretty wild town. A huge deposit of silver was found nearby. It was called the Comstock **Lode.** Gold was found in Virginia City, too.

Thousands of people rushed in to get rich. Wild, lawless mining camps sprang up. People were rowdy and got into fights. A few people made big fortunes. But most found nothing and didn't stay. The towns they left became **ghost towns.**

Strike up a tune! This banjo player performs at Virginia City's Crystal Saloon.

The U.S. government cut back on making silver money in the 1870s. Then many of Nevada's silver mines closed.

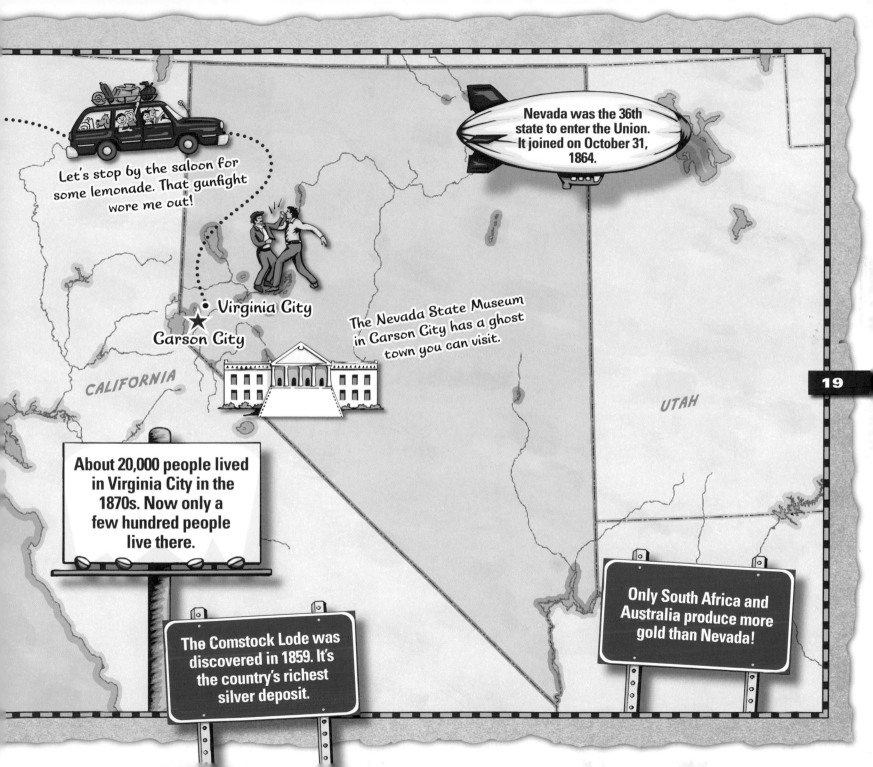

Let's stop by the saloon for some lemonade. That gunfight wore me out!

Nevada was the 36th state to enter the Union. It joined on October 31, 1864.

• Virginia City

★ Carson City

The Nevada State Museum in Carson City has a ghost town you can visit.

CALIFORNIA

UTAH

About 20,000 people lived in Virginia City in the 1870s. Now only a few hundred people live there.

The Comstock Lode was discovered in 1859. It's the country's richest silver deposit.

Only South Africa and Australia produce more gold than Nevada!

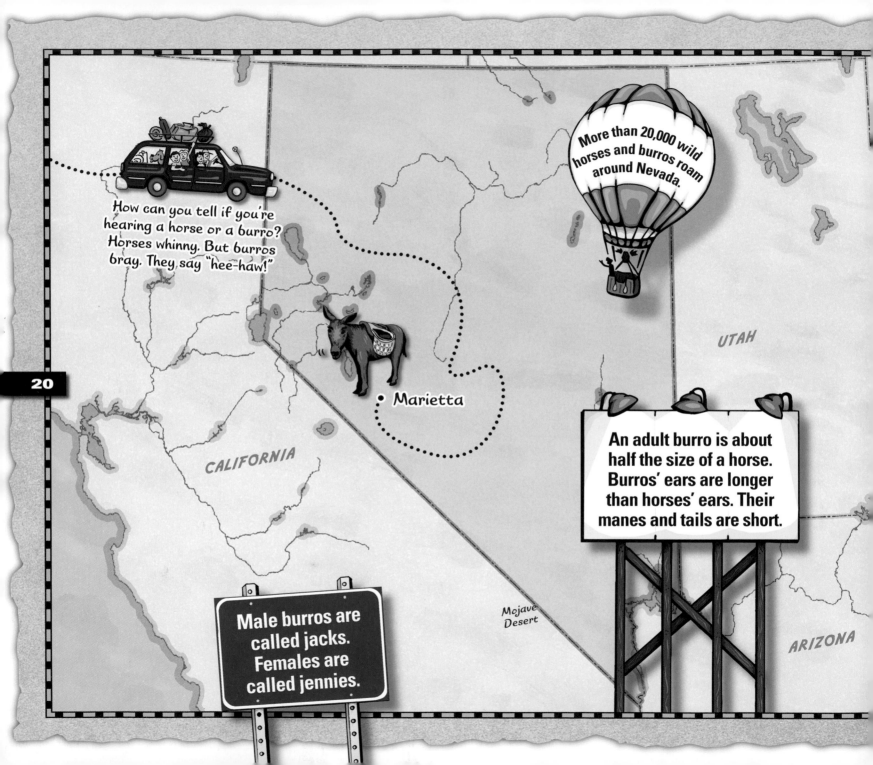

How can you tell if you're hearing a horse or a burro? Horses whinny. But burros bray. They say "hee-haw!"

More than 20,000 wild horses and burros roam around Nevada.

UTAH

20

• Marietta

An adult burro is about half the size of a horse. Burros' ears are longer than horses' ears. Their manes and tails are short.

CALIFORNIA

Mojave Desert

ARIZONA

Male burros are called jacks. Females are called jennies.

The Wild Burro Range in Marietta

Want to see herds of wild, free-roaming burros? Just head out to the Wild Burro Range! More than eighty wild burros live there.

A burro is a small donkey. Burros were useful in the Old West. They were used as pack animals. They are sure-footed on mountainous land.

Miners brought burros here in the late 1800s. The miners were looking for silver and gold. Some of the burros escaped. They had babies. Soon there was a big herd of wild burros!

Wild burros roam Nevada's Mojave Desert.

Would you like to adopt one of Nevada's wild horses or burros? Several sites in Nevada hold sales now and then.

Kick up your feet! Dancers perform at Elko's National Basque Festival.

Reno also holds a Basque festival every summer.

Elko's National Basque Festival

Big bulls gallop through the streets. Their hooves make a thundering sound! Ahead of them are fearless runners. Can they outrun the bulls?

What in the world are you watching? It's an event called Running from the Bulls! It opens the National Basque Festival.

Stick around. You'll see weight-lifting and wood-chopping contests. People are dancing in colorful costumes, too.

Basque **immigrants** arrived in California in the 1800s. They came from the mountainous Basque Region. It crosses the border between Spain and France. From California, they moved into Nevada. They still love to celebrate their **traditions**!

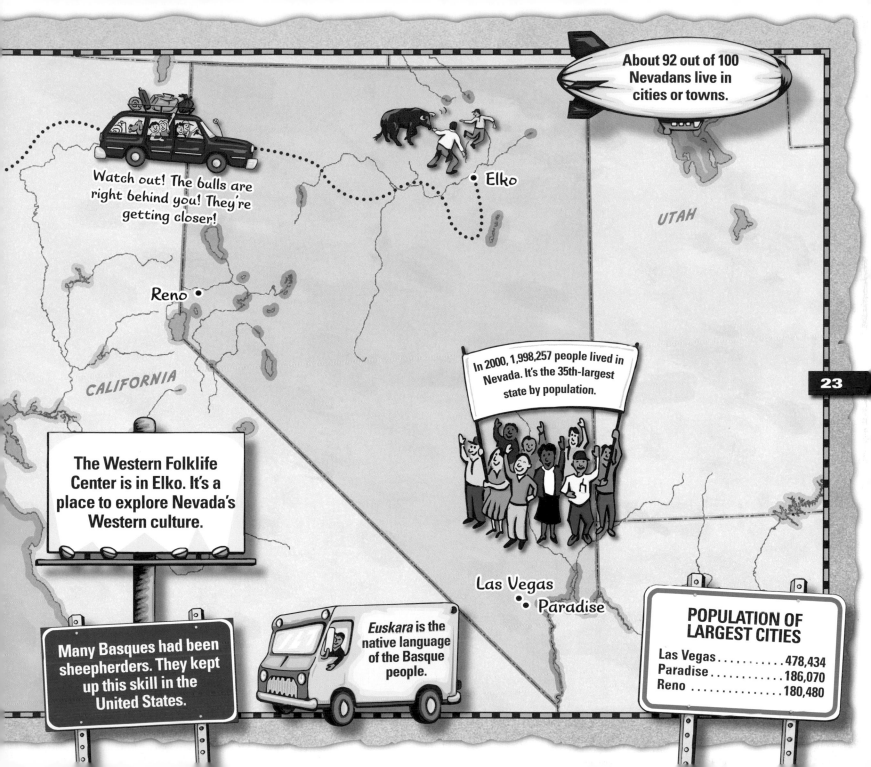

About 92 out of 100 Nevadans live in cities or towns.

Watch out! The bulls are right behind you! They're getting closer!

• Elko

UTAH

Reno •

In 2000, 1,998,257 people lived in Nevada. It's the 35th-largest state by population.

CALIFORNIA

The Western Folklife Center is in Elko. It's a place to explore Nevada's Western culture.

Las Vegas
•• Paradise

Many Basques had been sheepherders. They kept up this skill in the United States.

Euskara is the native language of the Basque people.

POPULATION OF LARGEST CITIES

Las Vegas 478,434
Paradise 186,070
Reno 180,480

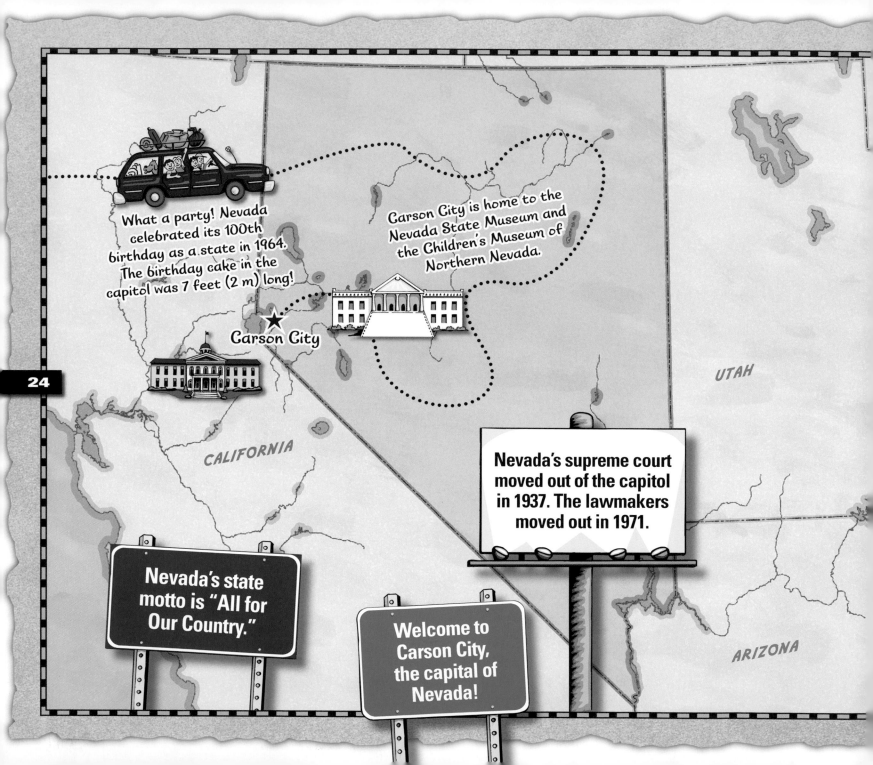

What a party! Nevada celebrated its 100th birthday as a state in 1964. The birthday cake in the capitol was 7 feet (2 m) long!

Carson City is home to the Nevada State Museum and the Children's Museum of Northern Nevada.

★ Carson City

UTAH

CALIFORNIA

Nevada's supreme court moved out of the capitol in 1937. The lawmakers moved out in 1971.

Nevada's state motto is "All for Our Country."

Welcome to Carson City, the capital of Nevada!

ARIZONA

The State Capitol in Carson City

The 2nd floor of the capitol has historical exhibits.

Nevada's state capitol is pretty old. State leaders began meeting there in 1871. This building is the center of state government.

Nevada's government has three branches. One branch consists of the state lawmakers. Another branch carries out the laws. The governor heads this branch. Judges make up the third branch. They decide whether laws have been broken.

Many newer buildings surround the capitol. The lawmakers meet in one building. The state's highest court meets in another. Only the governor's offices remain in the capitol.

Nevada's governor has offices in the capitol.

Listen to the water roar! Don't forget to stop by Hoover Dam!

Hoover Dam is in the Black Canyon of the Colorado River, near Boulder City.

Visiting Hoover Dam

Whoosh! The water thunders down from the dam. Take a tunnel to see the power plant. Or climb high on the deck. You'll see the river snaking into the distance. You're touring Hoover Dam!

Hoover Dam is one of Nevada's water projects. Many were built in the early 1900s. They all involve dams across rivers.

The dams have many benefits. They control floods and store water for **irrigation.** Some create lakes. Many dams provide **hydroelectric** power, too.

Hoover Dam stretches across the Colorado River. It was completed in 1936. Lake Mead backs up behind the dam. It's a great **recreation** spot!

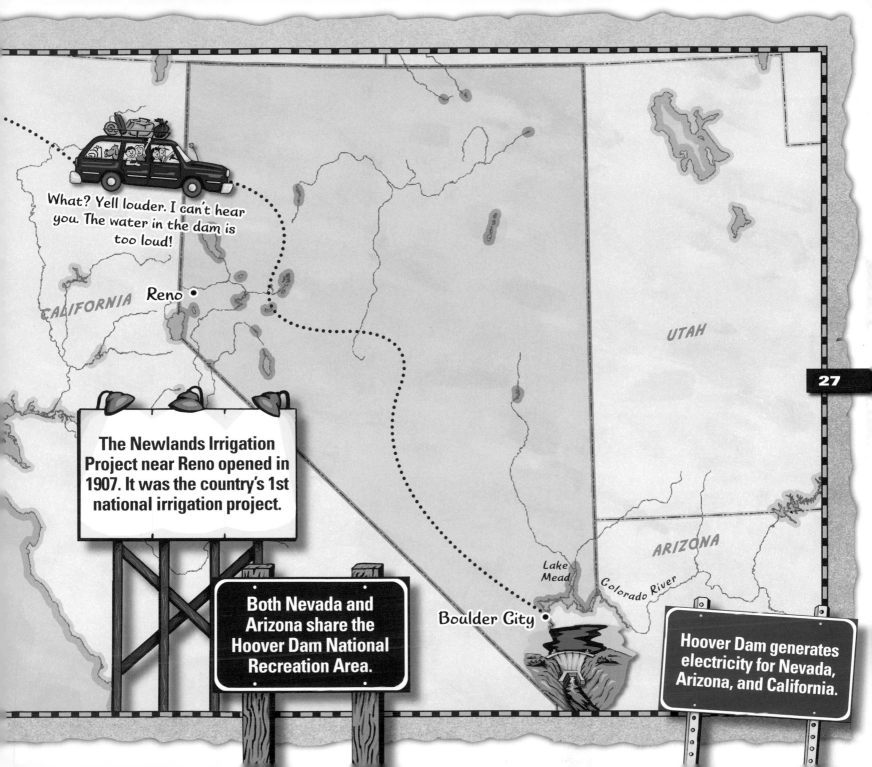

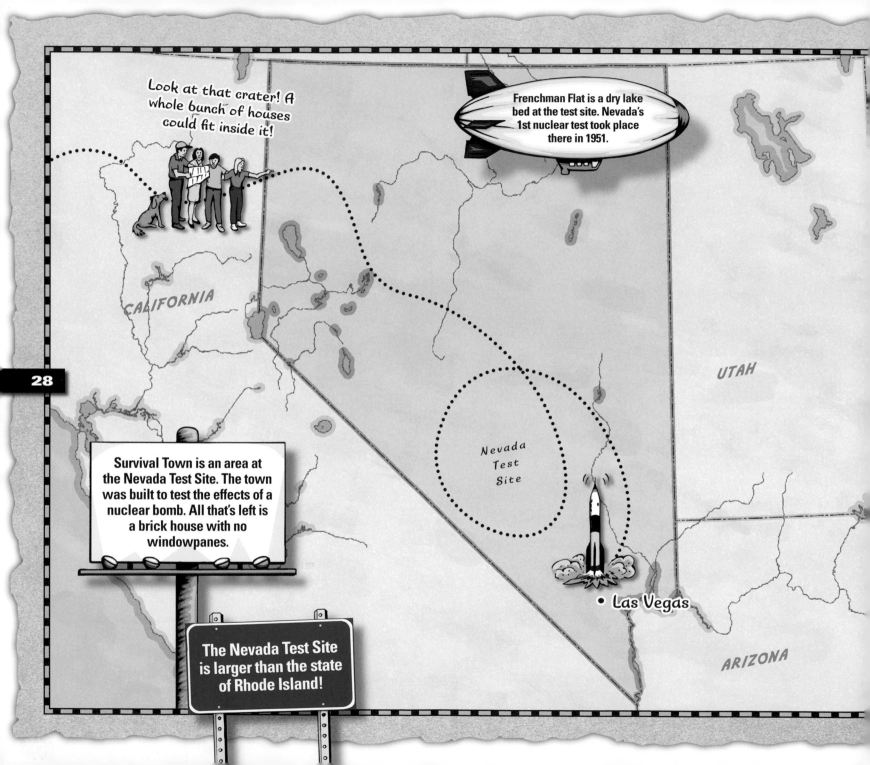

Look at that crater! A whole bunch of houses could fit inside it!

Frenchman Flat is a dry lake bed at the test site. Nevada's 1st nuclear test took place there in 1951.

CALIFORNIA

UTAH

Nevada
Test
Site

Survival Town is an area at the Nevada Test Site. The town was built to test the effects of a nuclear bomb. All that's left is a brick house with no windowpanes.

Las Vegas

ARIZONA

The Nevada Test Site is larger than the state of Rhode Island!

Touring the Nevada Test Site

It looks like an endless desert. You see massive holes in the ground. You pass a house with broken-out windows.

You're touring the Nevada Test Site. It covers a huge area northwest of Las Vegas. The U.S. government once tested **nuclear** weapons here.

The first test took place in 1951. A 1962 test created Sedan Crater. It's a huge hole made by explosives.

Nuclear tests stopped in 1992. Now the center does many kinds of studies. It tests rockets, weapons, and dangerous waste materials.

Glad this isn't your house? It was destroyed by a blast at the Nevada Test Site.

BEEF is the Big Explosives Experimental Facility. It's a test station at the Nevada Test Site.

Nevada's Lunar Crater

Want to save yourself a trip to the Moon? Just head to Lunar Crater instead!

Stand on the edge of the hole. It's more than twelve football fields wide! It looks like a giant **meteor** fell there. But it's actually where a volcano erupted. Then the volcano collapsed. That created the big hole. Now that hole is called the Lunar Crater! It's halfway between Ely and Tonopah.

What's a lunar crater? It's a bowl-shaped hole in the Moon's surface. Of course, this is not the Moon. But people thought the crater looked like the Moon.

The crater has a rough, rugged surface. In that way, it *is* like the Moon. Astronauts trained there in the 1960s. They were training to go to the Moon!

Cowboy Life at Soldier Meadows Ranch

Want to live the cowboy life? Just spend some time at Soldier Meadows Ranch. It's northeast of Gerlach. You can ride horses there. You can even work with the cowboys!

Ranching is the state's major farm activity. Nevada has hundreds of cattle and sheep ranches. These animals produce meat, milk, and wool. They have lots of grazing land in Nevada.

You'll find crops growing in the river valleys. Most crop farming is done with irrigation. In some areas, farmers pump water from underground. Hay is Nevada's top crop. And no wonder! The cattle need it for food.

Is the cowboy life for you? Just talk to a Nevada rancher!

Nevada's biggest rodeo is the National Finals Rodeo in Las Vegas every December.

Who needs casinos when you can visit AdventureDome?

Las Vegas, Reno, and Lake Tahoe are Nevada's major sites for casinos.

Las Vegas . . . for Kids!

Spend a day in the AdventureDome. You'll take thrilling roller coaster rides. You'll bang around in bumper cars. And you'll see clown acts and trapeze shows.

You're at Circus Circus! It's a big hotel in Las Vegas.

Tourism is Nevada's biggest industry. Many Nevada tourists come to Las Vegas. Grown-ups try to win money at **casinos** there. But Las Vegas has great places for kids, too.

Mandalay Bay is another fun hotel. You can walk through tunnels inside shark tanks. You'll really get close to the sharks! Eek!

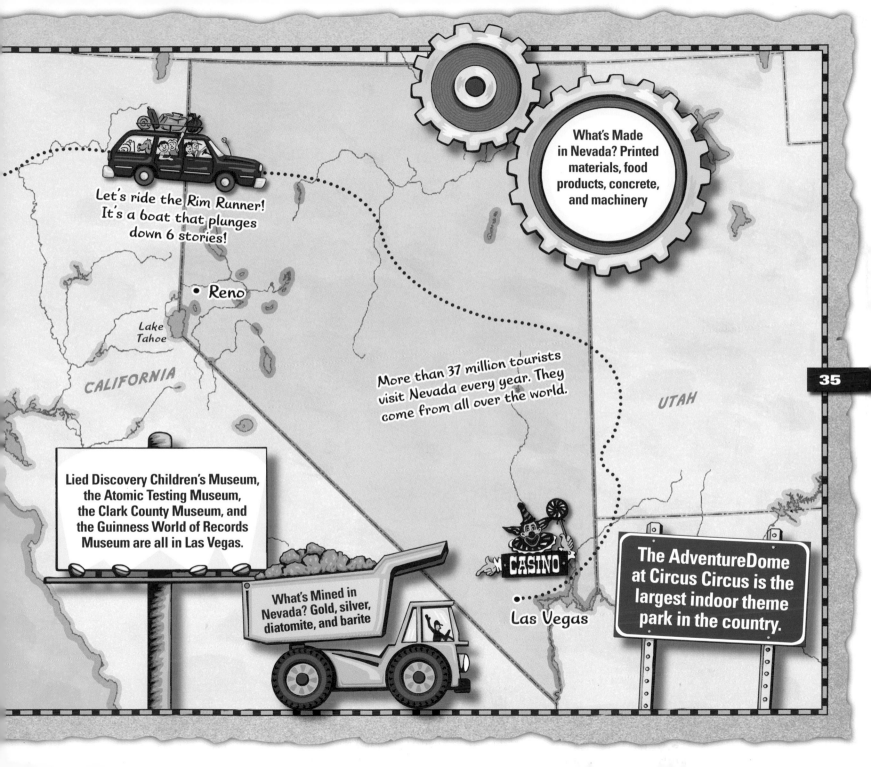

Let's ride the Rim Runner! It's a boat that plunges down 6 stories!

What's Made in Nevada? Printed materials, food products, concrete, and machinery

• Reno

Lake Tahoe

CALIFORNIA

UTAH

More than 37 million tourists visit Nevada every year. They come from all over the world.

Lied Discovery Children's Museum, the Atomic Testing Museum, the Clark County Museum, and the Guinness World of Records Museum are all in Las Vegas.

What's Mined in Nevada? Gold, silver, diatomite, and barite

CASINO

Las Vegas

The AdventureDome at Circus Circus is the largest indoor theme park in the country.

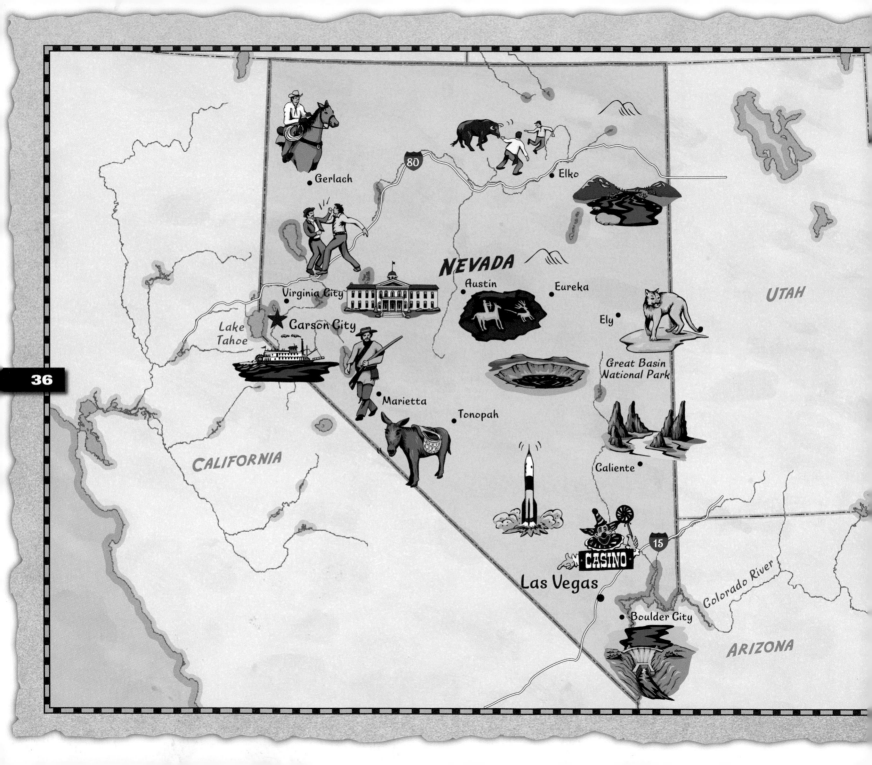

NEVADA

UTAH

CALIFORNIA

ARIZONA

Gerlach

Elko

Virginia City

Austin

Eureka

Ely

Great Basin
National Park

Lake
Tahoe

Carson City

Marietta

Tonopah

Caliente

CASINO

Las Vegas

Boulder City

Colorado River

80

15

OUR TRIP

We visited many amazing places on our trip! We also met a lot of interesting people along the way. Look at the map on the left. Use your finger to trace all the places we have been.

How old are the bristlecone pine trees in Great Basin National Park? See page 11 for the answer.

How many petroglyphs are in Sloan Canyon National Conservation Area? Page 14 has the answer.

What is the country's richest silver deposit? See page 19 for the answer.

What is another name for a male burro? Look on page 20 for the answer.

What is the native language of the Basque people? Page 23 has the answer.

For which states does the Hoover Dam produce electricity? Turn to page 27 for the answer.

How big is the Lunar Crater? Look on page 31 for the answer.

What is the country's largest indoor theme park? Turn to page 35 for the answer.

That was a great trip! We have traveled all over Nevada!
There are a few places we didn't have time for, though. Next time, we plan to visit the Fleischmann Planetarium and Science Center in Reno. Visitors can watch star shows and use telescopes. The center also features a large meteorite collection.

More Places to Visit in Nevada

WORDS TO KNOW

casinos (kuh-SEE-noze) places where people play games of chance to win money

ghost towns (GOHST TOUNZ) towns that are empty because everyone has moved away

hydroelectric (hye-droh-i-LEK-trik) relating to electric energy produced by water power

immigrants (IM-uh-gruhnts) people who leave their home country and move to another country

irrigation (ear-uh-GAY-shuhn) bringing water to fields through ditches or pipes

lode (LOHD) a deposit of rock that contains valuable metals

meteor (MEE-tee-ur) a rock that falls from space

nuclear (NOO-klee-ur) relating to the energy produced by splitting atoms

pioneer (pye-uh-NEER) one of the 1st settlers in an unsettled land

recreation (rek-ree-AY-shuhn) games, sports, or hobbies that people enjoy in their spare time

scout (SKOUT) someone who makes new trails through an unexplored area

traditions (truh-DISH-uhnz) long-held customs

tram (TRAM) a boxlike car that travels on overhead wires

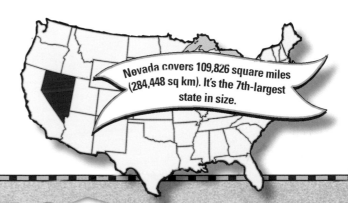

Nevada covers 109,826 square miles (284,448 sq km). It's the 7th-largest state in size.

STATE SYMBOLS

State animal: Desert bighorn sheep

State artifact: Tule duck decoy

State bird: Mountain bluebird

State fish: Lahontan cutthroat trout

State flower: Sagebrush

State fossil: *Ichthyosaur*

State grass: Indian rice grass

State metal: Silver

State precious gemstone: Black fire opal

State reptile: Desert tortoise

State rock: Sandstone

State semi-precious gemstone: Turquoise

State trees: Single-leaf piñon and bristlecone pine

State flag

State seal

STATE SONG

"Home Means Nevada"

Words and music by Bertha Raffetto

Way out in the land of the setting sun,
Where the wind blows wild and free,
There's a lovely spot, just the only one
That means home sweet home to me.
If you follow the old Kit Carson trail,
Until desert meets the hills,
Oh you certainly will agree with me,
It's the place of a thousand thrills.

Chorus:
Home means Nevada,
Home means the hills,
Home means the sage and the pine.
Out by the Truckee's silvery rills,
Out where the Sun always shines,
There is the land that I love the best,
Fairer than all I can see.
Right in the heart of the golden west
Home means Nevada to me.

Whenever the sun at the close of day,
Colors all the western sky,
Oh my heart returns to the desert grey
And the mountains tow'ring high.
Where the moon beams play in shadowed glen,
With the spotted fawn and doe,
All the livelong night until morning light,
Is the loveliest place I know.

(Chorus)

FAMOUS PEOPLE

Adams, Eva Bertrand (1908–1991), former director of the U.S. Mint

Agassi, Andre (1970–), tennis player

Alexander, Ben (1911–1969), actor

Ashurst, Henry Fountain (1874–1962), politician

Bentley, Helen Delich (1923–), journalist and politician

Bilbray, James Hubert (1938–), politician

Casey, James E. (1888–1983), founder of the United Parcel Service (UPS)

Cavanaugh, Hobart (1886–1950), actor

Clark, Walter van Tilburg (1909–1971), author

Dat-So Lu-Lee (ca. 1829–1925), American Indian basket weaver

Kramer, Jack (1921–), tennis player

Laxalt, Paul (1922–), politician

Laxalt, Robert (1923–2001), author

Maddux, Greg (1966–), baseball player

Nixon, Pat (1912–1993), former first lady of the United States

Purviance, Edna (1895–1958), actor

Reid, Harry M. (1939–), politician

Winnemucca, Sarah (ca. 1844–1891), American Indian author and reformer

Wovoka (ca. 1856–1932), American Indian religious leader

Zajick, Dolora (1952–), opera singer

TO FIND OUT MORE

At the Library
Coerr, Eleanor, and Darcie Park (illustrator). *S Is for Silver: A Nevada Alphabet*. Chelsea, Mich.: Sleeping Bear Press, 2004.

Fuchs, Bernie. *Ride Like the Wind: A Tale of the Pony Express*. New York: Blue Sky Press, 2004.

Rambeck, Richard. *Andre Agassi*. Chanhassen, Minn.: The Child's World, 1996.

Rambeck, Richard. *Greg Maddux*. Chanhassen, Minn.: The Child's World, 1997.

Siebert, Diane, and Wendell Minor (illustrator). *Sierra*. New York: HarperCollins, 1991.

On the Web
Visit our home page for lots of links about Nevada: *http://www.childsworld.com/links*

Note to Parents, Teachers, and Librarians: We routinely verify our Web links to make sure they are safe, active sites—so encourage your readers to check them out!

Places to Visit or Contact
Nevada Commission on Tourism
401 North Carson Street
Carson City, NV 89701
800/638-2328
For more information about traveling in Nevada

Nevada Historical Society
1650 North Virginia Street
Reno, NV 89503
775/688-1190
For more information about the history of Nevada

INDEX

Bye, Silver State.
We had a great time.
We'll come back soon!